YOUR KNOWLEDGE HAS VALUE

Yashwanth Kumar Rasani

Asean or China? ThyssenKrupp's best opportunities in oriental expansion

GRIN Publishing

Bibliographic information published by the German National Library:

The German National Library lists this publication in the National Bibliography;
detailed bibliographic data are available on the Internet at http://dnb.dnb.de .

Imprint:

Copyright © 2014 GRIN Verlag GmbH
Print and binding: Books on Demand GmbH, Norderstedt Germany
ISBN: 978-3-656-89417-9

This book at GRIN:

http://www.grin.com/en/e-book/289129/asean-or-china-thyssenkrupp-s-best-
opportunities-in-oriental-expansion

GRIN - Your knowledge has value

Since its foundation in 1998, GRIN has specialized in publishing academic texts by students, college teachers and other academics as e-book and printed book. The website www.grin.com is an ideal platform for presenting term papers, final papers, scientific essays, dissertations and specialist books.

Visit us on the internet:

http://www.grin.com/

http://www.facebook.com/grincom

http://www.twitter.com/grin_com

ASEAN OR CHINA?

THYSSENKRUPP'S BEST OPPORTUNITY IN ORIENTAL EXPANSION

THYSSENKRUPP AS A GROUP

ThyssenKrupp is one of the Europe's largest steel producers based in Duisburg & Essen, Germany. It is one of the Europe's largest conglomerates with more than 670 offices across 80 countries of the world. Not only steel, it is also a leader in manufacturing elevators, mechanical goods for automotive industry, marine systems and provides Business, IT and Real-Estate services alongside. Although ThyssenKrupp is present in many countries around the globe, its main sales come from Germany (33%) itself, followed by rest of the EU (28%) and NAFTA (21%). Apart from Germany, Spain & Italy alone constitute for about 9% of its sales revenue (ThyssenKrupp Group, http://www.thyssenkrupp.com/financial-reports/12_13). It is also a leader in innovation and expanding into Aerospace & Defense industries.

```
Group structure

Corporate Headquarter

ThyssenKrupp AG    Sales: 38.6 bn € (September 30, 2013)   Employees: 160,168

ThyssenKrupp Business Services
ThyssenKrupp IT Services
Real Estate

Business Areas

Components Technology              Materials Services
  Steering                           Metals Services
  Damper                             Special Materials
  Springs & Stabilizers              Special Services
  Automotive Systems
  Camshafts                        Steel Europe
  Forged & Machined Components       ThyssenKrupp Steel Europe
  Presta Camshafts                   Processing
  Bearings
  Undercarriages
                                   Steel Americas*
Elevator Technology                  CSA
  Central / Eastern / Northern Europe ThyssenKrupp Steel USA
  Southern Europe / Africa / Middle East
  Americas
  Asia / Pacific
  Access Solutions

Industrial Solutions
  Process Technologies
  Resource Technologies
  System Engineering
  Marine Systems
```

Figure 1: ThyssenKrupp`s fields of expertise (Source: ThyssenKrupp AG Communications)

THYSSENKRUPP IN ASIA

ThyssenKrupp is growing at a very fast pace in Asia-Pacific and currently holds a strong base in South Korea, India, China and Japan. For example, the company`s relationship with India dates back to 1860 A.D. and with Japan to Meiji restoration times in early 1900s. The group openly declared that it will concentrate more on Asia than ever before. The group already employs some 19000 people in diverse activities in the region. Most of the present day metros and bullet trains that operate in major cities of China, Korea and now in India are engineered & serviced by ThyssenKrupp. (ThyssenKrupp Asia Pacific, http://www.thyssenkrupp.com/en/international/asien/).

China has pushed down many countries in competition and has evolved as an economic powerhouse in the last few decades through its foresight, strategy and commitment. The world is stumbled upon by its amazing success and growth. Almost every multinational company in the world has set up (or) in process of setting up their branches in China to get access to a 1.4 billion people (approx) market and take advantage of its hard-working & low cost labor force, policies and vibrant consumerism. ThyssenKrupp is no exception. But, ASEAN which has come up as a united front in competition to the two major Asian lookouts, China & India will be a best opportunity bet for this German conglomerate?!

ASEAN

ASEAN stands for 'Association of South East Asian Nations'. It comprises of ten South- East Asian countries which are Myanmar, Thailand, Cambodia, Laos, Vietnam, Philippines, Indonesia, Brunei, Malaysia and Singapore. This region was once called "Indo-Chine" in ancient times and is a cultural link between Indian sub-continent and China. ASEAN initially started as an association for regional co-operation and empowerment and has been slowly emerging as a political & united socio-cultural identity. Its headquarters is located in Jakarta, Indonesia and is all set to become a one-market economy by 2015. So, from the end of 2015 onwards, we have to see ASEAN as one trade zone just like the EU. It is still expanding with new memberships on board like East Timor, Micronesia, Papua New Guinea and with Japan, China, India and Australia as observer nations. (ASEAN http://www.asean.org/)

ASEAN BASIC FACT SHEET

❖ *Seventh largest economy in the world and third in Asia after China & Japan giving tough competition to India.*

❖ *Highest visited tourist and expat destination in entire Asia*

❖ *Third most populous unit (after China and India)*

❖ *Largest under-water natural resources in Asia (E.g. Brunei, one of the largest exporters of natural gas)*

❖ *Second youngest population after India (60% under age 35) (ASEAN http://www.aseam.org/)*

3

REASONS WHY ASEAN IS A BETTER INVESTMENT ZONE COMPARED TO CHINA

Apart from the aforementioned ASEAN basic facts, the following reasons stand out in particular when it comes to an advantage over China in terms of FDI.

	WHY ASEAN?	**WHY NOT CHINA?**
Diversity	ASEAN is not a homogenous market like China. It has ten different nations with wide range of differences. Some of the languages are Thai, Malay, Balinese, Bahasa, Tagalog, Vietnamese, and Cebuano and so on. That is why; ASEAN is a better market for any European company to diversify risk.	Though China is a big country in size with vast natural resources, its population is pretty much monolithic. There are only two major languages in China, Mandarin and Cantonese. And cultural differences are not drastically different from region to region.
Economic Stability	After the 2008 financial crisis, ASEAN economy has been consistent and strong. In fact it has the lowest volatility recorded since 2000. (World bank data)	After the 2008 financial crisis, Chinese economy has actually slowed down and has become more volatile than before in the last decade.
Consumer Demand	ASEAN has been successful in reducing significantly the extreme poverty and it is still the no.1 in the world in GDP Per capita growth rate since 1970s. For example, Vietnam`s per capita income has doubled in just ten years from 1995 – 2006. (McKinsey & Co)	Though China is the largest economy in the world, its income differences are huge and its per capita income growth is still low.
Free Market Ideology & Partnerships	ASEAN is a highly pro-western market. Singapore is a good example of free trade ideology and it is the second most advanced city in the world (Global Competitiveness Report,	While China is highly government regulated economy and it has taken some serious stances against free market spirit over the recent times like banning Western social media companies and others including

4

	2014). Moreover, it has good trade links with EU and other strategic alliances including SAARC (South Asian Association for Regional Co-operation), TPP (Trans-Pacific Partnership)	*TPP alliance. It is even opposing the idea of ASEAN becoming a political & military force like that of NATO.*
Education	*ASEAN pedagogical skills are more sought out than China. All ASEAN countries were ex-colonies (except Thailand) and have one or more European language proficiency. For e.g. English language use in Singapore & Myanmar, Spanish language influence in Philippines. Due to this, European companies may not find difficulty in operating in ASEAN.*	*China is spending billions of dollars employing European teachers to acquire foreign language skills. Chinese education system is still predominantly a Mandarin speaking monolingual system.*
Geography	*ASEAN has three times its land size of sea area and is globally well positioned in the middle, acting as a bridge between Australasia, Japan and India/Middle East. It is highly rich in natural resources especially Oil and Natural gas which China lacks. For e.g., South China Sea has one of the richest self-sufficient under-water oil reserves.*	*China's 'sea-advantage' is less when compared to ASEAN and it is one of the largest importers of oil & gas in the world and its energy demand is still skyrocketing.*
Rate of return	*Unlike China, ASEAN does not suffer from housing bubble. Moreover, according to Global Connectedness Report by McKinsey, ASEAN ranks better than China in goods flow and global connectivity. ASEAN received more FDI than China in 2013 and is now the home for 227 MNCs with more than 1 billion $ revenue each. (McKinsey). The tax and*	*China's housing bubble is a major setback (60 million on edge of losing jobs in construction sector) and also the manufacturing sector in China has been slowing down in the recent years. (Time.com)*

other restriction policies are very loose which enable foreign investors to get high rate of return. For e.g., Singapore's tax relief program, Brunei's corporate tax abolishment and others.	

Table 1: Overall comparison between ASEAN and China

REASONS WHY ASEAN IS BETTER FOR THYSSENKRUPP

ThyssenKrupp has already begun to see Singapore as a strategic spot due to its location, resource availability and has made it as its Asian hub. Let's have a look how each ASEAN country is contributing to ThyssenKrupp in a unique way.

Country	Promising field for ThyssenKrupp	Comment
Singapore	All- round	Seventh largest sales in Asia Pacific. Regional headquarters of ThyssenKrupp is located here
Indonesia	Automotive	The fourth populous country and largest archipelago in the world has huge demand in automotive and electronics sector to better improve its transport connectivity in its 18000 islands. Almost 70% of diesel railway locomotives in Indonesia are from Essen. Moreover, the company is the top supplier of elevators here. (ThyssenKrupp Asia-Pacific)
Malaysia	Steel & Elevator	Malaysia has been known for

	Technology	its magnificent skyscrapers. Its real estate is in need for steel and ThyssenKrupp is already taking advantage of it.
Vietnam	Materials services	Vietnam is a good market for ThyssenKrupp`s service industry. Vietnam has got huge mineral reserves and ThyssenKrupp is pursuing the distribution, processing and warehousing activities of Steel, Copper, Aluminum and other metals here.
Philippines	Marine Systems	It's a niche market for ship building (4th best place in the world) due to its location and also the country is advancing into aerospace and defense industry rapidly. (Phil marine, 2015)
Thailand	Resource & Component Technologies	It's a niche market for Industrial Solutions in Asia Pacific. Due to its highly tropical nature and due to the presence of well connected inland-waterways with abundant mining reserves, it is standing out among all other ASEAN countries in terms of effective business area industrial management.

Cambodia, Myanmar and Laos are slightly lagging behind due to their stagnant economies and are often seen as weak spots in ASEAN. Nevertheless, they offer huge future potential for the ThyssenKrupp group. The group has its presence in Brunei & East Timor also especially in marine oil & gas exploration field technology.

Table 2: Analysis of each ASEAN country

Now, let's discuss how each business area of ThyssenKrupp in ASEAN has its advantage over China:

ThyssenKrupp's area of expertise	Why ASEAN?	Why not China?
Shipbuilding/Marine Systems	In spite of global downturn in this industry, SE Asia is still advancing due to its investor-friendly relations with the west. Large numbers of new ports are being constructed every year and major ports like Singapore, Jakarta are being expanded due to regional & international demand. Moreover, almost half of the region's population live by the sea.	China's shipbuilding industry is actually stagnated with many low-end harbors being closed down. Its ship sales have been falling down due to less competitiveness, quality and excess production.
Steel	Steel consumption is skyrocketing in ASEAN due to its buzzing automotive and real estate industries.	"China's steel is now as cheap as cabbage" is the headline of Market watch on Oct13, 2014. Due to oversupply of steel and slowdown in manufacturing sector has led to the falling prices. It is expected to continue for a long time according to reports.
Elevator technology		ThyssenKrupp is already operating in China and is doing well in this area so far. In fact, China is a leader in this area. But the real estate bubble in china is going to have a negative impact on this market. China has built some 36 million apartments of indemnification which are empty. (prnewswire.com)

| Industrial Solutions, Components & Materials Services | SE Asia has been a hub for components making since early 1900s. Japanese manufacturing companies have a long presence in this region. This region has been witnessing giant changes in income levels, urban population, telecom & social media expansion. This is one of the reasons why industry solutions have a great future in this region along with material services w.r.t its mineral reserves. It is one of the largest producers of cement, coal, natural gas, aluminum and so on. | Some of the problems associated with China:

1) Product reputation (Black market economy is huge in China when compared to SE Asia)

2) Less Safety (High government regulations)

3) Slowdown of manufacturing sector together with aggressive marketing techniques. (For e.g., Lenovo, Chinese computer brand and Xiaomi, the Chinese smart phone company are actually facing criticism in many countries including SE Asia due to China's efforts to push its brands on basis of extravagant publicity and over-satiable promotion |

Table 3: Comparison between ASEAN and China w.r.t business areas

CONCLUSION

By this analysis, we can say ThyssenKrupp has a promising future in ASEAN more than China. The recommendation to ThyssenKrupp is not to overlook China, but to take advantage of ASEAN for its diversified Asia-Pacific presence and profitability. The group has been indulged in numerous expansion activities in ASEAN than China lately. It is constructing new ports in Philippines, railway lines in Indonesia, Sky scrapers and steel plants in Malaysia, Mining towns in Thailand, Warehouses in Vietnam and Assembly units in Singapore for a better and prosperous future in the region that would contribute the best to both the region and the conglomerate itself.

BIBLIOGRAPHY

Springer, Jon, Mr. "ASEAN A Better Investment than China for Businesses and Investors." Forbes. Forbes Magazine, 30 Apr. 2014. Web.

"Integrated ASEAN Region Challenge China?" Wharton.upenn.edu, 15 June 2014. Web. http://knowledge.wharton.upenn.edu/article/

"Beyondbrics." Beyondbrics. Financial Times, n.d. Web. 02 Nov. 2014. http://blogs.ft.com/beyond-brics/

Tonby, Oliver, Vinayak HV, and Fraser Thompson. "Understanding Asean." http://www.mckinsey.com/insights/public_sector/ . McKinsey & Co, May 2014. Web.

ThyssenKrupp Asia-Pacific. ThyssenKrupp AG, n.d. Web. < http://www.thyssenkrupp.com/en/international/asien/>

(n.d.). Retrieved October 14, 2014, from http://www.aseanfoundation.org/

(n.d.). Retrieved November 1, 2014, from http://www.theguardian.com/world/2008/oct/21/china-globalrecession

Gross savings (% of GDP). (n.d.). Retrieved October 10, 2014, from http://data.worldbank.org/indicator/NY.GNS.ICTR.ZS

The Global Competitiveness Report 2014 - 2015. (n.d.). Retrieved October 17, 2014, from http://www.weforum.org/reports/global-competitiveness-report-2014-2015

Industry Facts. (n.d.). Retrieved November 2, 2014, from http://philmarine.com/post/18/Industry-Facts.html

Overview of ASEAN Steel Market. (n.d.). Retrieved October 30, 2014, from http://www.oecd.org/sti/ind/Item 6. OECD Steel Secretariat - Mr. Naoki Sekiguchi - July 2013.pdf

He, L. (2014, October 13). China steel now as cheap as cabbage, weighing on global price. Retrieved October 16, 2014, from http://www.marketwatch.com/story/china-steel-now-as-cheap-as-cabbage-weighing-on-global-price-2014-10-13

ASEAN shipping firms strong against global troubles; However ASEAN integration means many more ships. (n.d.). Retrieved November 1, 2014, from http://www.reedpanorama.com/asean-shipping-firms-strong-against-global-troubles-however-asean-integration-means-many-more-ships

China: No safe harbor for weak shipyards - Shipping Tribune. (n.d.). Retrieved October 16, 2014, from http://www.shippingtribune.com/china-no-safe-harbor-for-weak-shipyards/

11